THE
DRIVING FORCE
LIVING LIFE AT FULL SPEED

LOVELAND, COLORADO
group.com

Group resources actually work!

This Group resource incorporates our R.E.A.L. approach to ministry. It reinforces a growing friendship with Jesus, encourages long-term learning, and results in life transformation, because it's

Relational
Learner-to-learner interaction enhances learning and builds Christian friendships.

Experiential
What learners experience through discussion and action sticks with them up to 9 times longer than what they simply hear or read.

Applicable
The aim of Christian education is to equip learners to be both hearers and doers of God's Word.

Learner-based
Learners understand and retain more when the learning process takes into consideration how they learn best.

Visit **www.group.com**

Credits
Contributors: Kyle Petty, Karl Leuthauser
Executive Developer: Amy Nappa
Chief Creative Officer: Joani Schultz
Copy Editor: Daniel Birks
Art Director: Jeff A. Storm
Cover Art Designer: Jeff A. Storm
Print Production Artist: Greg Longbons
Production Manager: DeAnne Lear

Unless otherwise indicated, all Scripture quotations are taken from the *Holy Bible,* New Living Translation, copyright © 1996, 2004. Used by permission of Tyndale House Publishers, Inc., Carol Stream, IL 60188. All rights reserved.

ISBN 978-0-7644-3749-6
10 9 8 7 6 5 4 3 2 1   17 16 15 14 13 12 11 10 09

Printed in the United States of America.

For all speaking requests/inquiries, please contact:
Theresa J. Brown
Vice President, Washington Speakers Bureau
1663 Prince Street, Alexandria, VA 22314
703.684.0555 x1027 (phone)   703.299.4556 (fax)
www.washingtonspeakers.com

CONTENTS

FOREWORD

I accepted Jesus Christ into my life when I was 14 years old. I had an uncle, named Randy Owens, and one day when we were in Talladega, Alabama, an accident happened that took his life. I could not explain it. The dots did not connect. I could not understand how we could ride together to Talladega in a van but not be going back together. It turned my whole world sideways.

As soon as we got back in the van and started home up the road, I started praying. I didn't know what I was praying for or what I was praying about. Even though I had gone to Sunday school and vacation Bible school and had been around my parents and my grandmothers all my life, I never truly understood what it was like to ask Jesus Christ to come into your life. At some point my heart softened; I asked Jesus Christ to come into my life and was saved while praying in the van. All of a sudden there was a peace and an assurance that whatever had happened to Randy, he was in a better place. And I knew that as I moved forward, my life was going to be better.

I have not always been the greatest Christian in the world since that time, because we all stumble and we all fall. But asking Jesus Christ to come into my life has always been a huge moment in my life. When I look back, nothing is bigger than giving yourself and your life to Christ. There's nothing bigger in your life. When you put your faith and belief in Christ first, it seems like everything else falls into place. There are hard days, no matter what you do. But when you put your faith in Christ, he leads you in a new direction. Where he leads you, you don't know, but you need to follow. My life has been totally different since that time.

I think that the driving force behind who I am and what I do and how I act or how I react is Jesus Christ. It's my prayer for you that as you use this book and study God's Word, God will be the driving force in your life, too.

—Kyle Petty

INTRODUCTION

Kyle Petty decided to become a race car driver when he was just a boy. It probably wasn't a difficult decision, given that his father and grandfather were already famous for racing. He won his first major race before he was 20, and has been racing ever since. This Bible study takes an in-depth look at the winning principles, practices, and priorities from Petty's life, and applies them to your life.

The areas of focus you'll explore in this study are ones men relate to, such as relationships, ambition, and purpose. They're things Kyle Petty knows firsthand, and that he shares with readers who join this journey. You'll discover the principles that come from these areas of focus over the next six weeks.

Here's how this study works.

First, the study is meant to be done in a group setting—it could be a men's breakfast on Saturday morning, a group of teen guys who meet weekly, a small group meeting in a home or restaurant, or even a lunch group at work. It could even be a father and son exploring life lessons together. Everyone in your group will participate in discovering the principles of a life lived with purpose.

Second, you'll want to make sure everyone gets a copy of this book. We recommend your group has one copy of *The Power to Win DVD,* too. There's an opportunity to watch a segment of the DVD at the beginning of each session to see and hear real-life stories directly from Kyle.

Briefly, here's how the sessions break down.

Think About It

This time will be spent thinking about a few key questions. A simple experience will help you walk through your thoughts on the topic. Then you'll talk about the connections you made to your life.

Talk About It

During this section, you'll take the question for the session a little deeper. The discussion here will tie your life connections to the Bible passages in the next section. This is an important time to get to know other guys' hearts and walk with each other through this discovery.

Study It

This section will challenge you as you dig into God's Word. It's a time where you can see the principles you discover exemplified in the Bible. You'll connect your discussion and experiences from before to your discoveries in different passages through further discussion and sharing.

Live It

This brings the study full circle. Just as you started the session reflecting on your life, you'll have a chance to reflect again as you connect what you've taken from the study to your life. The activities will guide you in making these connections.

Commit to It

Before you conclude your session, it's important to commit to an action point that will help you continue to grow. We'll give you three options to choose from.

SESSION 1

Focused Relationships

Showing the way by following the Father

WHAT EACH PERSON WILL NEED:

- ❯ Bible
- ❯ Pen
- ❯ Photos from his wallet, cell phone, or PDA
- ❯ *The Driving Force* book

If you have *The Power to Win* DVD, watch from the beginning to 4:25 minutes where Kyle talks about his racing heritage. After the video, discuss this question with your group: **What's one insight you gained from what Kyle shared?**

Think About It (15 minutes)

 Car numbers 43 and 45 have been powered by an enduring tie that is stronger than sponsorship, cup victories, or even crews. Numbers 43 and 45 have been tied together through the bond of family. The Petty racing patriarch, Lee Petty, won the very first Daytona 500 in 1959 and earned three Grand National titles. Lee's son, Richard, was the most-winning racer in NASCAR history. Richard's son, Kyle, scored eight victories on the NASCAR Nextel Cup circuit, and has built a business that has become one of the most successful in motor sports history. When Kyle's son, Adam, made his professional racing debut at Peach State Speedway in 1998, he became the first fourth-generation professional athlete in the United States.

For four generations, the fathers in the Petty family pointed the way for their sons in integrity, focus, and passion for racing. Each son received a passion that Kyle's mom, Lynda, once remarked, "simply gets into each son's blood."

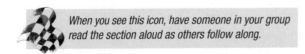

When you see this icon, have someone in your group read the section aloud as others follow along.

Pass your books around the room, and have each person write his name, phone number, and e-mail address in the spaces provided on pages 74-77 of this book.

For better or for worse, your father gave you an example to follow or reject. His choices have had a large impact on who you've become and the choices you've made in turn. Rather than getting stuck in what has been, this study will ask you to consider how your example will affect those around you in the future. Your father may have set you up for success or left you to fend for yourself. Either way, it's up to you to decide. Will you spend the remainder of your life as a man who propels others into the life and challenge God has for them, or will you be a hindrance and hurdle others must overcome to find and fulfill their purpose and calling?

Think for a moment about the example your father gave you (or is giving you). Was it the sort of example you would want to pass on to your children or others around you? Think of one specific memory or example that shows a quality your father had that you want to emulate. For example, your father's work ethic may have been demonstrated in your memory of him going to work before anyone else in the family woke up. Write the example here:

_____

_____

_____

Now think of one specific memory that shows a flaw or deficiency your father had that you hope to overcome. For example, your father's overemphasis on work may have been demonstrated when he missed an important event in your life.

_____

_____

_____

10

If some of your group members haven't met, make sure you each share your name and the reason you came to this group. Then have each person share one memory of how his father or another man made a positive impact in his life.

Talk About It (15 minutes)

Discuss:

❯ What does it require for us to set a positive example for our children or for others around us?

❯ What roadblocks or hazards can get in the way as we try to set that example?

❯ How can we overcome those roadblocks?

If you have children, you are setting an example for your kids. And if you don't have children, you are setting an example for the people you connect with.

Form pairs. With your partner, discuss the example you're setting in each of the following areas. Rank each area, with 10 being an extremely positive example and 0 being an extremely negative example.

Living honestly and with integrity

0	1	2	3	4	5	6	7	8	9	10

Putting God first in my life

0	1	2	3	4	5	6	7	8	9	10

Treating my wife (or others) with love and respect

0	1	2	3	4	5	6	7	8	9	10

Making myself available to my kids (or friends in need)

0	1	2	3	4	5	6	7	8	9	10

Working diligently using my gifts and skills

0	1	2	3	4	5	6	7	8	9	10

After pairs have had about five minutes to talk over their rankings, read the following together:

After the regular races of the NASCAR season, the Chase begins. During the Chase, the 12 top-ranked drivers have all the points they accumulated throughout the year reset to 5,000 (with some minor changes for the wins they had). In effect, it's kind of like a restart button for the year. The remainder of the season dictates how they finish the Chase, regardless of whether they were ranked first or 12th when the Chase began.

God's grace is kind of like the Chase. No matter what's been done to you or what you've done, you can start setting an example for your kids or others today. In effect, God keeps us all in the race to make a difference no matter how far we've fallen behind.

Have men return to their pairs to discuss:

> ❯ Is there any area in your life where you would like to change the example you've been setting? How are you going to start making that change?

> ❯ Have you experienced God's grace for a restart in any area of your life? What happened?

USELESS TRIVIA

Many NASCAR drivers have won back-to-back titles. Only one driver has won a third consecutive title. Who holds the record?

Study It *(20 minutes)*

No matter where we've come from or what we've done, we have two things in common: None of our fathers were perfect men and none of us are perfect men. We all have something to learn when it comes to setting an example for future generations. The good news is that we have a perfect example to follow.

Read Romans 8:11-13:

The Spirit of God, who raised Jesus from the dead, lives in you. And just as God raised Christ Jesus from the dead, he will give life to your mortal bodies by this same Spirit living within you. Therefore, dear brothers and sisters, you have no obligation to do what your sinful nature urges you to do. For if you live by its dictates, you will die. But if through the power of the Spirit you put to death the deeds of your sinful nature, you will live.

Discuss:

❍ What does this passage say about the negative examples that we have been given?

❍ What does it say about the areas of our lives where we have been a bad example?

❍ How do we go about changing sinful patterns, behaviors, and examples in our own lives?

Read Romans 8:14-17:

For all who are led by the Spirit of God are children of God. So you have not received a spirit that makes you fearful slaves. Instead, you received God's Spirit when he adopted you as his own children. Now we call him, "Abba, Father." For his Spirit joins with our spirit to affirm that we are God's children. And since we are his children, we are his heirs. In fact, together with Christ we are heirs of God's glory. But if we are to share his glory, we must also share his suffering.

Discuss:

❯ How does being a child and heir of God affect the approach you might take in being an example to your children or others?

❯ How does or can God show us what it means to be a good example as a father and as a man?

Let's take a moment to look at the example that God has given us as a Father. For each of the areas below, list how God acts toward his children versus predominant examples you witness on earth.

God's Example	*Earthly Examples*
Patience and dependability	
Ability to help	
Ability to love	
Approach toward discipline	
Feelings toward you	
Other differences	

Discuss:

❯ What aspect of God's character and example is most difficult for you to grasp?

❯ In what way do you want to be more like your heavenly Father?

USEFUL TRIVIA

Jesus called God "Abba," which means Father or Daddy. In fact, the word "Abba" is used three times in the New Testament. Can you find these Scripture passages?

Live It (10 minutes)

Get in groups of two to four. Find pictures in your wallet, PDA, or telephone of your loved ones. Try to find the most important people in your life. For each person, write down his or her name and how you plan to be a God-like example to that person:

Person 1:

Person 2:

Person 3:

Person 4:

Person 5:

Find a partner and tell him one thing you're going to do differently as a result of this study.

Commit to It

Before you conclude this session, choose to complete one of the action points that follow, an action point that came out of the study, or another action point you come up with. Commit to completing the action point before your next meeting, and be prepared to share what happened or what you learned.

Option 1: Read Matthew 7:9-11. Ask God to show you how he is different from your earthly father.

Option 2: Make a positive memory with your child (or, if you don't have children, another child in your life such as a niece or nephew). Rather than having them do something *you* like to do, do something you know your *child* will enjoy. Spend the extra time and money needed to make it unforgettable.

Option 3: Write a note or letter to your dad thanking him for the example he gave you.

IN THE GARAGE

SESSION NO.

SESSION TITLE

Use this page for additional notes and thoughts on this week's session.

FOR PERSONAL USE | DATE:

SESSION 2

Focused Ambition

Balancing ambition, humility, and courage

WHAT EACH PERSON WILL NEED:

> ❥ Bible
>
> ❥ Pen
>
> ❥ *The Driving Force* book

If you have *The Power to Win* DVD, watch from 4:25 minutes to 5:54 minutes where Kyle talks about his competitive nature. After the video, discuss this question with your group: **What's one insight you gained from what Kyle shared?**

Think About It (15 minutes)

 Kyle Petty is a winner on many levels. He oversees one of the most successful motor sports businesses in history, has won eight professional races, has placed in the top 10 over 170 times, and has brought in more than $30 million in race earnings through his driving. He has the drive to compete and the focus to succeed.

It's important, however, to remember that Kyle has started over 800 races he didn't win and has had over 650 starts where he failed to finish in the top 10. Much of Kyle's success is found in his dogged determination not to give

> *Complete a quick check-in regarding the commitments you made at the end of the last session. Let each person share how he followed through and any insights gained.*

up. Setbacks and disappointments are regular companions on the road to success. If we can't live with failure, we'll never find success.

Think for a moment about some of your greatest accomplishments and most spectacular failures. In the space provided below, list a time you took the *checkered flag*—when you had an unforgettable victory in your life. Perhaps it came in a sports

19

 *When you see this icon, have someone in your group read the section aloud as others follow along.*

event you participated in, a business deal you closed, or a breakthrough you had with your wife or kids, or in another relationship.

Then list a time you caused or experienced a *yellow flag* in your life. The situation or your efforts caused a wreck that affected others around you. You might include a time you accidentally insulted a client, fouled out of a game, or lost it while you were driving friends or family on a busy highway.

Finally, list a time you felt like you *failed to qualify* for the race. For example, you may have been cut from a team, demoted at work, or shot down for a date.

Checkered Flag Moment:

Yellow Flag Moment:

Failed to Qualify:

With a partner, discuss the following:

❯ What do the moments you wrote about have in common? What's different about them?

❯ What part did your attitude play in any of the moments you wrote about?

❯ Pick one of the moments you wrote about and explain what you would do differently if you could do it again.

Talk About It (15 minutes)

Contrary to widely held beliefs, the Bible never declares ambition to be sinful. It warns us against *selfish* ambition. It clearly speaks against using others, lying, or cheating to get ahead. And the Bible gives strong warnings against greed. But the men and women who made a difference for God's kingdom were full of ambition. Their ambition was focused on the kingdom of God, and they submitted to God's will. Consider the following examples:

- Elijah wasn't timid or apologetic when he challenged the prophets of Baal (see 1 Kings 18).
- Paul wasn't weak-willed or halfhearted when he shared the good news with the Gentiles (see 2 Corinthians 11:23-27).
- Jesus wasn't without passion in the mission he came to accomplish (see Luke 22:44 and John 5:19).

Scripture calls us to be humble and gentle. At the same time it also calls us to be strong, courageous, and faithful. We were created to strive, grow, and accomplish. And everyone wants their striving to count and to be effective.

Discuss:

- When is it wrong or sinful to be competitive?

- Do you think competition is an important part of the Christian life? Why or why not?

- When can competition be God-honoring?

As a group, create a list that offers some guidelines for God-honoring competition. In the "God-Honoring Competition" column listed below, write down the attitudes, strategies, and characteristics of God-honoring competition. In the "Ungodly Competition" column, write down attitudes, strategies, and characteristics that lead to unhealthy competition.

God-Honoring Competition	*Ungodly Competition*

Study It (15 minutes)

Form pairs. With your partner, play three quick games of Rock, Paper, Scissors. (Fast review: Paper covers rock. Rock crushes scissors. Scissors cut paper.) If you're not sure how to play, someone else in your group can show you how. If you're really competitive, you can play for the best four out of seven. With your partner, discuss:

❷ How important was it for you to win this quick game?

● What is something you're striving for in your life right now that is extremely important to you?

> *"Each time he said, 'My grace is all you need. My power works best in weakness.' So now I am glad to boast about my weaknesses, so that the power of Christ can work through me. That's why I take pleasure in my weaknesses, and in the insults, hardships, persecutions, and troubles that I suffer for Christ. For when I am weak, then I am strong."*
> *—2 Corinthians 12:9-11*

● How is your approach toward that area in your life different from your approach to the Rock, Paper, Scissors game you just played? Why is it different?

● What will it take for you to "win" in the important area you described?

In a recent interview with Sporting News, racing great Mario Andretti said, "Desire is the key to motivation, but it's determination and commitment to an unrelenting pursuit of your goal—a commitment to excellence—that will enable you to attain the success you seek."

Read 1 Corinthians 9:24-27:

Don't you realize that in a race everyone runs, but only one person gets the prize? So run to win! All athletes are disciplined in their training. They do it to win a prize that will fade away, but we do it for an eternal prize. So I run with purpose in every step. I am not just shadowboxing. I discipline my body like an athlete, training it to do what it should. Otherwise, I fear that after preaching to others I myself might be disqualified.

● How would you describe your desire, determination, and commitment when it comes to serving God?

● Why do you think Paul (the author of 1 Corinthians) had such tremendous desire, determination, and commitment to God and God's plans?

❯ How would your life change if it had the same focus as Paul's?

❯ What do you think God might be calling you to focus your ambition, desire, and determination on?

❯ How can you give God everything you've got?

Live It (15 minutes)

Imagine you had a real shot at winning the Chase for the Cup with a purse of about $5 million—that you were one of the 12 top-qualifying drivers at the end of the regular racing season. Now imagine you were one victory away from securing a Cup victory. What would you do to win? How much time, energy, and focus would you give toward the race?

Consider the following reality. What value would the $5 million have to you on the day of your death? How important would winning the Chase be to you after 10,000 years in heaven? How much would the $5 million purse be worth to you after 100,000 years in eternity?

If you ever have a chance to win the Chase, go after it with all you've got! But you have a chance to go after a prize that is way bigger than the Chase for the Cup. Every person you lead to a relationship with Jesus will be affected by your efforts forever. Every person you encourage to grow closer to God, to reach out to others, or to keep pushing through hard times will feel the impact of your efforts for all eternity. There is no prize that is more valuable, more important, or more deserving of your ambition, desire, and determination than the prize of advancing God's kingdom here on earth.

Make a racing strategy and plan for how you can advance God's kingdom. Read Matthew 6:19-21 (below), and then take few minutes to prayerfully consider each of the following areas where you can make a forever difference. Then go after the prize with all you've got!

"Don't store up treasures here on earth, where moths eat them and rust destroys them, and where thieves break in and steal. Store your treasures in heaven, where moths and rust cannot destroy, and thieves do not break in and steal. Wherever your treasure is, there the desires of your heart will also be."

❍ People in my life who need the good news of Jesus:

❍ Some ways I can build relationship with those people:

❍ Ways I can serve in my local church:

❍ Christians I know who need encouragement:

❍ Injustices or pain that I can help change:

Pick one of the areas from the previous page that you know God is asking you to do. Find a partner and share with him what you need to do and how you're going to do it.

Commit to It

Before you conclude this session, choose to complete one of the action points that follow, an action point that came out of the study, or another action point you come up with. Commit to completing the action point before your next meeting, and be prepared to share what happened or what you learned.

Option 1: Follow up on more than one of the items in the racing strategy you created in the "Live It" section of today's session. You have the publisher's permission to photocopy that page and post it wherever you need to for it to serve as a reminder.

Option 2: Make an individualized definition of winning when it comes to the things of God's kingdom. For example, winning may mean leading your uncle to a relationship with Jesus, turning a co-worker from an enemy into a friend, or mentoring three kids in your youth group.

Option 3: Develop and start following a training regimen for the race you are in. Your regimen could include daily Scripture reading and prayer, attending regular worship services at church, or finding other ways to connect with God.

IN THE GARAGE

Use this page for additional notes and thoughts on this week's session.

FOR PERSONAL USE   DATE:

SESSION 3

Focused Purpose

Finding and fulfilling God's plan for your life

WHAT EACH PERSON WILL NEED:

- Bible
- Pen
- *The Driving Force* book

If you have *The Power to Win* DVD, watch from 5:55 minutes to 7:53 minutes where Kyle talked about the impact the Petty family has had on racing. After the video, discuss this question with your group: **What's one insight you gained from what Kyle shared?**

Think About It (15 minutes)

 Lee, Richard, Kyle, and Adam Petty have all made their own mark on racing. Lee was a pioneer in racing with many impressive firsts. Richard was one of the most-winning drivers of all time. Kyle has directed Petty Enter-

Complete a quick check-in regarding the commitments you made at the end of the last session. Let each person share how he followed through.

prises with skill and is known for his charitable endeavors. Adam was a rising star, competing in his first professional NASCAR race at the age of 18!

Despite the racing heritage and expectations of fans and the media, each Petty was allowed to make his own way and find his own purpose. God didn't need four Richards or four Kyles. God needed only one Lee, one Richard, one Kyle, and one Adam. And God needs only one of you. Your specific gifts, calling, and purpose are different from those around you. Only you can touch the lives of those whom God has put before you to make an impact on. Ephesians 5:1 tells us to "imitate God." Other than that, we must be ourselves if we are to accomplish the unique call God has put on each of our lives.

Each person should grab four similar items that fit in his hand and get in a circle with several others. For example, if you're meeting at a restaurant, have each man grab four toothpicks. You can also use coins, coffee stir sticks, or scraps of paper.

Read each of the four statements below. If a man agrees with the statement, he should drop a toothpick (or whatever item he has in his hand) into the middle of the circle. If not, he should do nothing. After each statement, allow whoever wants to share his thoughts or feelings about the statement to do so.

1. My purpose in life is very clear to me.
2. I feel like I'm on track for the course God has for my life.
3. I sometimes feel crippled by the expectations or demands that others have of me.
4. I feel like I am in control of my destiny and future.

In the circles, discuss:

❯ Did anyone feel any apprehension or frustration about "showing his hand" during this exercise? Explain.

❯ When is it most difficult for you to be who you really are? When is it easy?

❯ Have you ever experienced a pull, desire, or demand that tempted you to live as someone other than who you really are?

Talk About It (10 *minutes*)

 To understand your purpose, you have to know who you are. Circle one of the words in each pair below that better describes who you are.

I am more:

Passionate	Levelheaded
Artistic	Rational
Leader	Servant
Verbal	Mathematical
Entrepreneurial	Managerial
Athletic	Musical
Spiritual	Practical
Creative	Committed
Loyal	Instinctive
Encouraging	Admonishing
Driven	Laid-back
Life of the party	Loner
Courageous	Cautious
Free-spirited	Organized
Playmaker	Planner
Responder	Thinker

Find a partner and share your list with him. With your partner discuss:

❯ What surprised you or jumped out at you as you went through this list?

❯ From what you know of your partner and what you see on *his* list, what are some things you think God may be asking him to do?

❯ What do *you* think God has gifted or is gifting you to do?

❯ Have you been faithful in using those gifts? Explain.

USEFUL TRIVIA

Paul wrote three different lists of spiritual gifts in his letters. Ephesians 4:11 contains one list. Can you find the other two lists? *Rom 12: 3-8, 1 Corinth 12:1 - 31*

Study It (15 minutes)

In pairs, read Ephesians 2:10:

For we are God's masterpiece. He has created us anew in Christ Jesus, so we can do the good things he planned for us long ago.

Discuss:

❯ What does this passage say about your calling and purpose?

❯ What would you say to someone who says he doesn't think God really has a purpose for his life?

Last week we touched on the fact that Jesus was focused on the mission he had for his time on earth. Let's take a moment to look closely at that mission and consider how it applies to our lives.

Read Luke 4:16-21:

When he came to the village of Nazareth, his boyhood home, he went as usual to the synagogue on the Sabbath and stood up to read the Scriptures. The scroll of Isaiah the prophet was handed to him. He unrolled the scroll and found the place where this was written:

"The Spirit of the Lord is upon me,
   for he has anointed me to bring Good News to the poor.
He has sent me to proclaim that captives will be released,
   that the blind will see,
that the oppressed will be set free,
   and that the time of the Lord's favor has come."

He rolled up the scroll, handed it back to the attendant, and sat down. All eyes in the synagogue looked at him intently. Then he began to speak to them. "The Scripture you've just heard has been fulfilled this very day!"

Then discuss:

❯ Why do you think Jesus relied on God's Spirit to fulfill his purpose even though Jesus is God?

❯ How do you know that God's Spirit is upon you for the work he's calling you to do? (See John 14:16-17.)

Write your name in the blank on line 1 in the personalization of Luke 4:18-19 on page 34 of your *The Driving Force* book. Then discuss with your partner:

❯ What gift or talent do you think God is asking you to use for his glory?

Write that gift or talent on line 2. For example, you could write, "for he has anointed me to **build and do construction**" or to "**encourage people who are discouraged**." Then discuss with your partner:

❷ Who do you think God is asking you to share that gift or talent with?

Write the group, person, or people on line 3. For example, you could write, "He has sent me to go on **short-term missions in Mexico**" or to "**serve in children's ministry at church**." Then discuss with your partner:

❷ What do you hope will change because of your work and service?

Write the change on line 4. For example, you could write, "that the **poor in Mexico will experience his love**" or "that the **children can see an example of a man who loves God**."

Personalization of Luke 4:18-19

1. The Spirit of the Lord is upon _____,
   your name

2. for he has anointed me to _____.

3. He has sent me to _____,

4. that the _____, and that
   the time of the Lord's favor has come.

Live It (20 minutes)

 Your personalized Luke 4:18-19 may be a purpose statement for the rest of your life. Or perhaps it is a specific purpose God is guiding you to in the near future. It is no accident that those words are written in your study guide. God has put those things in your heart and is bringing them out for you to go after.

The passage Jesus fulfilled said that he was anointed to do what God called him to do. Those who God calls, he empowers. You are not only gifted to fulfill your purpose, but you have been given special favor and position or "anointing" to complete it. It may not happen this week or this year, but don't stop moving toward your purpose.

Allow each person to read his personalization of Luke 4:18-19 aloud. Then spend a little time as a group affirming God's call in each person's life. You might comment on how his personality fits with the statement, how you have seen him do similar things in the past, or how you hope his purpose is fulfilled. Pray as a group for each person after you have shared your thoughts with him.

Commit to It

Before you conclude this session, choose to complete one of the action points that follow, an action point that came out of the study, or another action point you come up with. Commit to completing the action point before your next meeting, and be prepared to share what happened or what you learned.

Option 1: God has a plan and purpose for everyone's life. But we all ultimately have one purpose. Find out what that purpose is by reading Matthew 22:37-40. Then think and pray about how you can fulfill that purpose.

Option 2: If you're not sure what God is calling you to do, just find a need at your local church and fill it. Try something new and see what happens! You may find through working with the youth group that you aren't called to work with teenagers in the long run, but that you love mentoring and leading small groups—and you'll get to change lives while you figure it out!

Option 3: If you want to find out more about who you are, consider taking a personality inventory. You might learn something from free tests on the Internet, but you're likely to learn much more from an inventory that has been vetted through research such as the Myers-Briggs Type Indicator or the DISC Profile.

IN THE GARAGE

SESSION NO. | SESSION TITLE

Use this page for additional notes and thoughts on this week's session.

FOR PERSONAL USE | DATE:

SESSION 4

Focused Through Loss

Allowing God into the hurt and difficulties in our lives

> **WHAT EACH PERSON WILL NEED:**
>
> ❯ Bible
>
> ❯ Band-Aid™
>
> ❯ Pen
>
> ❯ *The Driving Force* book

If you have *The Power to Win* DVD, watch from 7:54 minutes to 12:11 minutes where Kyle talks about losing his son, Adam. After the video, discuss this question with your group: **What's one insight you gained from what Kyle shared?**

Think About It (15 minutes)

 It was the day everything changed for Kyle and Pattie Petty. Only one month earlier, their son, Adam Petty, had made his NASCAR Winston Cup Series debut at Texas Motor Speedway. The 19-year-old had already begun making his mark, so fans and racing insiders were full of anticipation and expectation.

On a Friday afternoon, Adam was 45 minutes into his practice session for the NASCAR Busch Series Grand National Division race. With only 15 minutes left in the practice, Adam approached turn 3 of the 1.058-mile oval when

Complete a quick check-in regarding the commitments you made at the end of the last session. Let each person share how he followed through.

something went wrong. No one knows what happened for certain, but the marks on the track indicated that the throttle stuck. Petty's car rode the concrete wall in turns 3 and 4 for 200 yards and caught fire as it came to a stop. After the accident, Adam was transported to Concord Hospital where he died from trauma to the head.

Is there a day in your life when everything changed? Perhaps you lost a parent, child, or friend. Maybe your world turned upside down when your parents divorced or you lost your job. It doesn't matter how it compares to the loss of others—whether it seems small or large, fresh or long ago. What matters is that it happened in your life and things wouldn't go back to how they were.

Grab a Band-Aid and open it up. On the cloth portion of the bandage, write one word that symbolizes the loss you experienced. For example, you could write "Mom" or "accident." Then stick the Band-Aid on your arm. Write your thoughts to the following questions in the space provided:

❯ What changed in your life on that day?

❯ What was the most difficult part of the loss when it happened?

❯ What's the most difficult part of the loss right now?

Talk About It (10 minutes)

Consider the Band-Aid on your arm right now. In many ways, it's a surprisingly accurate representation of grief. When we experience loss, it remains close to us for a long time—always touching us in some way like the cotton of the Band-Aid. Others may be aware of the loss, but no one completely sees or understands how it affects us—it is somewhat hidden to the rest of the world. Finally, we all deal with loss in different ways. Some of us move through grief quickly with a strong outpour of emotion, like tearing a Band-Aid off with a sharp sting. Others of us remove it slowly, exposing parts of our wound as we can bear it. Still others keep it covered, waiting for time to slowly wear it away.

There's really no "normal" way to grieve loss. The most important thing is that we allow grief to happen when it comes and we keep pushing forward when we feel we can't go on. With two or three other men, discuss:

❷ How do you typically deal with disappointment and loss?

❷ Is there an area of loss or disappointment in your life that you are currently working through or need to work through? How is it affecting you in this season of your life?

❷ Is there anyone you care about who is working through grief, loss, or disappointment right now?

❷ How can you help and support that person?

USELESS TRIVIA

The Chevy Malibu averages 32 miles per gallon on the highway. How many gallons of fuel does a race car burn per 2.5-mile lap at the Indianapolis Motor Speedway?

Study It (15 minutes)

As Kyle describes the moments he and his family shared just after Adam's death, he talks about how his family came together and prayed, and then prayed some more. He remarks, "We came to the conclusion that day...that there were two directions we could take. We could be extremely bitter and hate everybody and everything. Or (we could) look at it and say we were very thankful to have this child that we had for 19 years. As we prayed, we came to the conclusion that we were very blessed."

The same choice is before you right now. Whether you have dealt with a tragic loss or a small setback, it's up to you to decide if you're going to become bitter or respond in thankfulness.

Form groups of four to discuss the following:

Read 1 Thessalonians 5:16-18:

Always be joyful. Never stop praying. Be thankful in all circumstances, for this is God's will for you who belong to Christ Jesus.

❷ Why do you think thankfulness is God's will for you?

❷ It's often difficult to feel or express thankfulness in the middle of a difficult situation. What should we do in the middle of those times?

❷ Think for a moment about the situation written on your Band-Aid. Is there anything you can find to be thankful for regarding that situation?

Write a word or two on the outside of your Band-Aid that represents that area of thankfulness. For example, you could write, "time" for the time you had with your mom, or "family" for the way your family grew closer together during that time.

Read 2 Corinthians 4:8-10:

> We are pressed on every side by troubles, but we are not crushed. We are perplexed, but not driven to despair. We are hunted down, but never abandoned by God. We get knocked down, but we are not destroyed. Through suffering, our bodies continue to share in the death of Jesus so that the life of Jesus may also be seen in our bodies.

● How does this passage apply to the difficulties and loss you've faced?

● How have you seen this passage play out in the bigger picture of your life?

● Describe a time in your life when your only option or strategy was to just keep moving forward through difficulty. How did you make it through that time?

● How can the life of Jesus be shown through the loss you wrote on your Band-Aid?

Live It (20 minutes)

In your same group of four, discuss:

● How has the loss or disappointment you've discussed throughout this session affected your beliefs or attitudes about God, yourself, or others?

❯ If God were sitting here and talking with you right now, what do you suppose he would say to you about the loss and disappointments you've faced?

Six years after losing his son, Kyle Petty remarked that the loss never completely goes away. But after two years, it became more bearable. Take your Band-Aid off your arm right now and hold it in your hand. While you hold it, talk to God silently about the issue. You may want to ask God to touch your heart where you feel loss. You may need help to go on another day, or you may just need to let go of an attitude, thought, or belief that came out of the situation. When you're done talking with God, hold your hand out in front of you and let the bandage fall to the ground as a symbol of your readiness to let go and allow God to come into that area of your life.

Commit to It

Before you conclude this session, choose to complete one of the action points that follow, an action point that came out of the study, or another action point you come up with. Commit to completing the action point before your next meeting, and be prepared to share what happened or what you learned.

Option 1: One of the most effective tools in working through loss and grief is simply to talk about what you've been through. If your heart is heavy or angry due to loss, find a friend, pastor, or counselor who you can talk to.

Option 2: Put a Band-Aid in your Bible as a reminder to be thankful in difficult times and to invite God into your grief and frustration. When you find a passage that speaks to you about thankfulness or God's care for you, write the reference on the Band-Aid.

Option 3: Start a journal so you can track your progress and growth through this difficulty. Begin every entry by writing at least two things you are thankful for. Over time, look at previous entries to see where God has taken you.

IN THE GARAGE

SESSION NO.

SESSION TITLE

Use this page for additional notes and thoughts on this week's session.

FOR PERSONAL USE | DATE:

SESSION 5

Focused Service

Reaching out to those in need

If you have *The Power to Win* DVD, watch from 12:12 minutes to 14:54 minutes where Kyle talks about his work with Victory Junction. After the video, discuss this question with your group: **What's one insight you gained from what Kyle shared?**

Think About It *(15 minutes)*

 Some professional athletes are known for dirty tactics, temper tantrums, or starting brawls during or after the event. Some are known for the run-ins they have with law enforcement, their relentless bragging or self-promotion, or their disregard for the safety and welfare of others. In the high-temptation, high-pressure atmosphere of fame, fortune, and success, it's refreshing to find a competitor who's known for working to meet the needs of others.

Complete a quick check-in regarding the commitments you made at the end of the last session. Let each person share how he followed through.

In response to Adam's death, Kyle and Pattie Petty launched Victory Junction Gang Camp. The mission of Victory Junction is to "enrich the lives of children with chronic medical conditions or serious illnesses by providing life-changing camping experiences that are exciting, fun, and empowering, in a safe and medically sound environment." Kyle has worked tirelessly to empower Victory Junction to meet its mission. For well over a decade, Kyle has led hundreds of NASCAR drivers, celebrities,

and other bikers on a motorcycle Ride Across America that has raised more than $10 million for Victory Junction and other children's charities.

While self-promotion and ego have become synonymous with professional sports, Kyle is living out the life-changing words of Christ in Matthew 25:40, "I tell you the truth, when you did it to one of the least of these my brothers and sisters, you were doing it to me!" Kyle has taken this passage literally and has chosen to spend much of his time and resources helping people who could never pay him back.

Think about the "least" of the people you come into contact with or have a desire to reach. Each of the spheres below represents a different sphere of influence in your life. In each sphere, or area of people you connect with, write down the people who might be considered the least. For example, you could write "Ted, the janitor" in your work sphere.

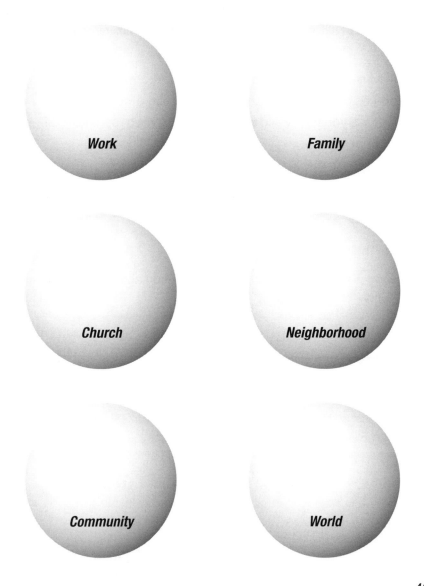

Talk About It (15 minutes)

When Victory Junction was being built, Kyle Petty explains, "Every obstacle we thought we'd come up against…they all just fell away. The place (came) up out of the ground in about 18 months." Once the Pettys set their minds to making a difference in the lives of kids with chronic illness, there was no stopping them. The vision grew and the resources they needed fell into place.

If you're determined to reach the least in any area, you will run into obstacles, but you won't be stopped. You will find a way to make a difference if you decide to do so.

Find a partner, and then share what you wrote on page 49 regarding the spheres of influence you have. Help each other brainstorm points of action. As you talk, write one thing you can do to make a difference in each sphere.

Read Proverbs 3:27:

> Do not withhold good from those who deserve it when it's in your power to help them.

Discuss the following questions:

❯ How does this passage apply to the ideas you and your partner came up with?

❯ Why do we often overlook the least?

❯ Which of the things that you wrote down do you feel most compelled to follow up on? What are you going to do?

Study It (15 minutes)

Not everyone is called to launch a camp like Victory Junction. Not everyone is called to work in a homeless shelter. But all Christians are called to bring justice and mercy when it is in their power. The "least of these" in your life can be a forgotten child in your neighborhood, a co-worker most people avoid, or a starving child in another country. Proverbs 3:27 tells us, "Do not withhold good from those who deserve it when it's in your power to help them." If you have noticed someone who is lost, broken, or forgotten, it is highly likely that you *can* do something about it.

Form groups of four. Then read Micah 6:8:

> No, O people, the Lord has told you what is good, and this is what he requires of you: to do what is right, to love mercy, and to walk humbly with your God.

Discuss:

❷ How are justice, mercy, and humility connected? Why do you think Scripture lists these three things as the requirements God has for us?

❷ How are acting justly, loving mercy, and walking humbly lived out in our lives?

❷ Talk about a time you overlooked someone who needed help. Compare that to a time you extended justice and mercy to someone in need.

Read Isaiah 58:4-7:

"What good is fasting
    when you keep on fighting and quarreling?
This kind of fasting
    will never get you anywhere with me.
You humble yourselves
    by going through the motions of penance,
bowing your heads
    like reeds bending in the wind.
You dress in burlap
    and cover yourselves with ashes.
Is this what you call fasting?
    Do you really think this will please the Lord?

"No, this is the kind of fasting I want:
    Free those who are wrongly imprisoned;
       lighten the burden of those who work for you.
    Let the oppressed go free,
       and remove the chains that bind people.
Share your food with the hungry,
    and give shelter to the homeless.
Give clothes to those who need them,
    and do not hide from relatives who need your help.

Then look at your spheres of influence on page 49. Discuss:

❯ How do verses 6-7 apply to your life right now?

❯ According to this passage, what is important to God? Why do you think it's so important to him?

Read James 1:27:

Pure and genuine religion in the sight of God the Father means caring for orphans and widows in their distress and refusing to let the world corrupt you.

❯ How does this passage contradict or reinforce what Christians spend the majority of their time and energy doing?

- On a scale of 1 to 10, where 10 is "right where God wants me" and 1 is "haven't even thought about it," how would you say these passages are playing out in your life?

- Do you believe God is calling you to reach out to an individual, a local group, or a distant people? Explain.

USEFUL TRIVIA

The prophet Micah predicted numerous events. He prophesized the downfall of Jerusalem and the destruction of the Temple by the Babylonians (which came to pass around 586 B.C.). Micah also envisioned the coming of the Messiah. What other prophet predicted the birth of Jesus?

Live It (20 minutes)

When Adam Petty turned 14, Kyle gave him a stock car chassis. "It was just the chassis," Adam recalls. "He told me to put together the sponsorship, get the parts, and build the thing myself." It took two years, but Adam did it. When it comes to extending mercy and justice and reaching the least, we're in a very similar situation. God has given us a chassis—a place to start. It's up to us to start putting the car together. Scripture says that every good thing comes from God and that we need to rely on him to make a real difference. But God is relying on us to make the effort. Let's use the metaphor of building a car to think about how we will reach the least of these in our spheres of influence. As you consider the possibilities, don't be afraid to dream big!

If the men in your group have difficulty thinking about how they can make a difference as individuals, consider working through this exercise as a group to create a plan for how you can make a difference together.

1. The chassis is the foundation of the car. Everything rests on the chassis. In your effort to serve, the chassis could be your idea or the people or person you are being called to serve. Write your idea here.

2. The suspension connects the car to its wheels. What will it take to make a real connection that will be meaningful to the people or person God has called you to reach? Write your method of meaningful service here.

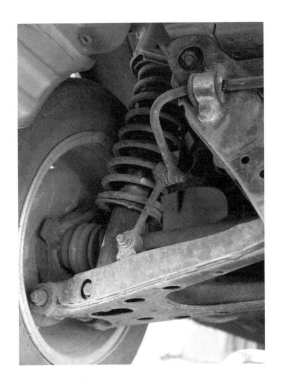

3. The motor gives the car power. How will you fund your idea, find the time for it, or call others to it?

4. NASCAR racing cars have impressive safety features including roll cages, harnesses, and even roof flaps to keep the car from gaining lift in an accident. There are always hazards to reaching out to others. If you're going to make a difference for the long term, you'll need to stay safe. What backup plans or safety systems should you put in place?

In your group of four, share the idea you're building. Then discuss these questions:

❷ What do you hope to accomplish through your efforts? How will you define success?

❷ What obstacles do you think you'll encounter?

❷ Who do you know who may be able to help you make a difference in this area?

Commit to It

Before you conclude this session, choose to complete one of the action points that follow, an action point that came out of the study, or another action point you come up with. Commit to completing the action point before your next meeting, and be prepared to share what happened or what you learned.

Option 1: The first step in helping the oppressed and hurting is to see them. Ask God to give you eyes to see the pain and hurt around you. Then ask him to show you how you can make a difference.

Option 2: God may not be asking you to start something new. Rather, he may be asking you to join something that's already going. Prayerfully consider which ministries at your church are meeting the needs of the "least of these," and join the effort.

Option 3: Sometimes our good-intentioned efforts to help others are counterproductive. For example, many experts discourage giving handouts to people who beg on the street. They encourage givers to contribute to agencies that have more effective screening methods. If you have the desire to reach someone in a specific demographic or population group, get counsel and advice from someone who is experienced in working with that group.

- ❯ Meals On Wheels Association of America
- ❯ Interfaith Hospitality Networks
- ❯ The DOE Fund Inc
- ❯ Habitat For Humanity
- ❯ National Coalition for the Homeless (Directory of Local Homeless Service Organizations)
- ❯ My Friends Place
- ❯ The Shelters and Soup Kitchens Directory
- ❯ The Salvation Army
- ❯ Homeless Shelter Directory
- ❯ Homeless Shelters Yahoo Directory
- ❯ Poverty Organizations Yahoo Directory
- ❯ World Vision
- ❯ Water Missions International
- ❯ Blood Water Mission
- ❯ Living Water International

IN THE GARAGE

Use this page for additional notes and thoughts on this week's session.

FOR PERSONAL USE | DATE:

SESSION 6

Focused Salvation

Making Jesus the center of our lives

> **WHAT EACH PERSON WILL NEED:**
>
> ❯ Bible
>
> ❯ Pen
>
> ❯ *The Driving Force* book

If you have *The Power to Win* DVD, watch from 14:55 minutes to 19:33 minutes where Kyle talks about his relationship with Jesus. After the video, discuss this question with your group: **What's one insight you gained from what Kyle shared?**

Think About It *(10 minutes)*

 Kyle Petty is the first to admit that he's not a perfect Christian. But he's also ready to explain that Christ has made all the difference in his life. He explains, "I accepted Jesus into my life when I was 14 years old...Nothing is bigger than giving yourself and giving your life to Christ. It seems like everything else falls into place."

The decision to follow Jesus takes just an instant, but the impact of that decision plays out for the rest of our life. At some point, we must decide if we want Jesus to become a part of our life. We then need to decide if we want Jesus to be just a part

Complete a quick check-in regarding the commitments you made at the end of the last session. Let each person share how he followed through.

of our life or the very center of our life. And even after we've invited Jesus to be the center of our life, he graciously brings to our attention various areas in our life that we haven't really yet yielded to him, but which he wants to be Lord of. Think for a while about the place Jesus has in each of the following areas of your life. To you, is Jesus an interesting idea, a part of your life, or Lord over all?

Mark an X at the point on each of the lines below that accurately describes your situation, and then write your answer to each question in the blank provided.

1. In my family life, Jesus is:

0	1	2	3	4	5	6	7	8	9	10

A non-factor   An important part   The most important part   The very center

This is seen in the way I

2. In my financial life, Jesus is:

0	1	2	3	4	5	6	7	8	9	10

A non-factor   An important part   The most important part   The very center

This is seen in the way I

3. In my work life, Jesus is:

0	1	2	3	4	5	6	7	8	9	10

A non-factor   An important part   The most important part   The very center

This is seen in the way I

4. In my thought life, Jesus is:

0	1	2	3	4	5	6	7	8	9	10

A non-factor   An important part   The most important part   The very center

This is seen in the way I

5. In my life, Jesus is:

0	1	2	3	4	5	6	7	8	9	10

A non-factor   An important part   The most important part   The very center

This is seen in the way I

Talk About It (15 minutes)

Jesus is either who he said he is—God among us who came to die for our sin—or he was crazy. The logical response is to believe what he said and give our entire life to him or to completely reject him. Trying to live a meaningful Christian life without making Jesus the center is like showing up to a NASCAR race with a go-cart. If this life is really about preparing for eternity, then there's no other option than to follow after Jesus with everything we've got.

Find a partner and discuss:

❯ Who do you think Jesus is? How does your life reflect that belief?

Share with your partner what you marked for each of the five areas on pages 61-62.

❯ Which, if any, of the areas are you most dissatisfied with?

❯ What changes would you like to see? What will it take for those changes to take place?

Look again at the five areas. With your partner, discuss what difference, if any, relying on Christ made in each area. Then discuss:

❯ Why is it important to make Jesus the center of every aspect of life?

❯ How do we go about making Jesus the center?

Study It (20 minutes)

Scripture says that "when we display our righteous deeds, they are nothing but filthy rags" (Isaiah 64:6). It really doesn't matter if we are "good" or "bad" people. We've all sinned; we've all done things we're ashamed of. And the only way we can come to God in our current state is through Jesus. Romans 10:9 says, "If you confess with your mouth that Jesus is Lord and believe in your heart that God raised him from the dead, you will be saved."

This is the first of a multitude of promises God gives us when we decide to follow Jesus and make him the center of our lives. In fact, 2 Corinthians 1:20 says, "For no matter how many promises God has made, they are 'Yes' in Christ" (New International Version). Let's take a moment to look at some of the promises that come with following Jesus.

Form groups of three or four to work through the following questions and passages:

1. Matthew 28:20

   Teach these new disciples to obey all the commands I have given you. And be sure of this: I am with you always, even to the end of the age.

   ❯ What promise does God give us?

   ❯ How have you seen this promise in your life?

   ❯ What would change if you relied more on this promise?

2. Matthew 6:31-33

"So don't worry about these things, saying, 'What will we eat? What will we drink? What will we wear?' These things dominate the thoughts of unbelievers, but your heavenly Father already knows all your needs. Seek the Kingdom of God above all else, and live righteously, and he will give you everything you need."

❯ What promise does God give us?

❯ How have you seen this promise in your life?

❯ What would change if you relied more on this promise?

3. John 3:14-16

And as Moses lifted up the bronze snake on a pole in the wilderness, so the Son of Man must be lifted up, so that everyone who believes in him will have eternal life. "For God loved the world so much that he gave his one and only Son, so that everyone who believes in him will not perish but have eternal life.

❯ What promise does God give us?

❯ How have you seen this promise in your life?

❯ What would change if you relied more on this promise?

4. John 14:27-28

   I am leaving you with a gift—peace of mind and heart. And the peace I give is a gift the world cannot give. So don't be troubled or afraid. Remember what I told you: I am going away, but I will come back to you again. If you really loved me, you would be happy that I am going to the Father, who is greater than I am.

   ❯ What promise does God give us?

   ❯ How have you seen this promise in your life?

   ❯ What would change if you relied more on this promise?

5. 2 Corinthians 5:17

   This means that anyone who belongs to Christ has become a new person. The old life is gone; a new life has begun!

   ❯ What promise does God give us?

   ❯ How have you seen this promise in your life?

   ❯ What would change if you relied more on this promise?

Live It (10 minutes)

Kyle Petty explains, "When you put your faith in Christ, that's the day that your whole life, your whole world, turns into a different direction. Where it leads you, you don't know, but you need to follow." Your life can go in a different direction right now if you make the same decision Kyle made when he was 14. Or if you've already decided to put your faith in Christ, today can be the day that you start getting serious about your faith or go deeper in it. Decide which of the following you want to do, and circle your decision.

❯ I am making a decision today to start following Christ.

❯ I am making a decision today to invite Jesus to be the center of my life instead of just a part of my life.

❯ I am making a decision today to move deeper in my relationship with Jesus.

❯ I have decided that I'm not interested in making a decision at this time.

Now find a partner and show him what you decided and explain why you made that decision. Tell your partner what you think that decision means for your life. Conclude this session and this study by praying for your partner and the decision he made.

Commit to It

If you have decided to start following Jesus, congratulations! You have started a joyful journey that will continue forever. Jesus promises that he will help us and that he will give us peace. But he never said that our lives automatically become easy when we start to follow him. In order to keep moving forward in your relationship with Jesus, consider the following:

- Get an easy-to-understand Bible (such as the New Living Translation or the New International Version). Start reading in the book of John.

- If you're not part of a local church, join one as soon as possible.

- Tell the pastor about the decision you made. Then ask the pastor what it means to be a follower of Christ and how baptism fits in with your decision.

- Commit to a small group or a men's group that will help you continue to grow in your faith.

If God has used this study to strengthen, inspire, or challenge you, consider using *Quiet Strength Men's Bible Study.* It's a men's Bible study very similar to this one that's based on the life and insights of Superbowl-winning coach, Tony Dungy.

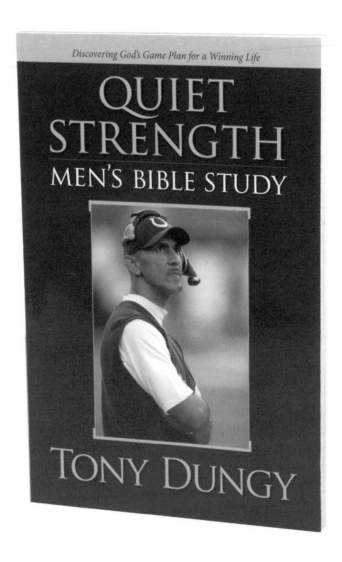

IN THE GARAGE

| SESSION NO. | SESSION TITLE |

Use this page for additional notes and thoughts on this week's session.

| FOR PERSONAL USE | DATE: |

TRIVIA ANSWERS

Session 1 Useful Trivia Answer
Mark 14:36
Romans 8:15-16
Galatians 4:6

Session 1 Useless Trivia Answer
Cale Yarborough

Session 2 Useful Trivia Answer
The Isthmian Games took second place to the Olympics. These Greek games were named after the isthmus upon which Corinth was situated.

Session 2 Useless Trivia Answer
A NASCAR pit crew has seven people. Their roles include the front tire changer, the front tire carrier, the rear tire changer, the rear tire carrier, the jack man, the gas man, and the gas catch can man.

Session 3 Useful Trivia Answer
1 Corinthians 12:1-31 and Romans 12:3-8

Session 3 Useless Trivia Answer
The closest finish in NASCAR history happened at the Darlington Raceway on March 16, 2003, when Ricky Craven beat Kurt Busch by .002 seconds.

Session 4 Useful Trivia Answer
Paul was a tentmaker.

Session 4 Useless Trivia Answer
A race car burns approximately 1.3 gallons of fuel per lap at the Indianapolis Motor Speedway.

Session 5 Useful Trivia Answer
The prophet Isaiah predicted the birth of Jesus. Read his predictions in Isaiah 7:14 and 9:6-7.

Session 5 Useless Trivia Answer
The Daytona 500

Session 6 Useful Trivia Answer
Paul wrote the letter to the Romans while he was in Corinth. In fact, Romans was written before Paul had ever been to Rome. Paul eventually visited Rome when he was taken there as a prisoner around A.D. 59-62.

Session 6 Useless Trivia Answer
A yellow strip across the rear of a NASCAR race car signifies a rookie driver.

Contacts

Name...Phone............................E-mail..

Name...Phone............................E-mail..

Name...Phone............................E-mail..

Name...Phone............................E-mail..

Name...Phone............................E-mail..

Name...Phone............................E-mail..

Name...Phone............................E-mail..

Name...Phone............................E-mail..

Name...Phone............................E-mail..

Name...Phone............................E-mail..

Name...Phone............................E-mail..

Name...Phone............................E-mail..

Name...Phone............................E-mail..

Name...Phone............................E-mail..

Name .... Phone .... E-mail ....

Name .... Phone .... E-mail ....

Name .... Phone .... E-mail ....

Name .... Phone .... E-mail ....

Name .... Phone .... E-mail ....

Name .... Phone .... E-mail ....

Name .... Phone .... E-mail ....

Name .... Phone .... E-mail ....

Name .... Phone .... E-mail ....

Name .... Phone .... E-mail ....

Name .... Phone .... E-mail ....

Name .... Phone .... E-mail ....

Name .... Phone .... E-mail ....

Name .... Phone .... E-mail ....

Name...Phone..............................E-mail...

Name...Phone..............................E-mail...

Name...Phone..............................E-mail...

Name...Phone..............................E-mail...

Name...Phone..............................E-mail...

Name...Phone..............................E-mail...

Name...Phone..............................E-mail...

Name...Phone..............................E-mail...

Name...Phone..............................E-mail...

Name...Phone..............................E-mail...

Name...Phone..............................E-mail...

Name...Phone..............................E-mail...

Name...Phone..............................E-mail...

Name...Phone..............................E-mail...

Name..	Phone......................................	E-mail...
Name..	Phone......................................	E-mail...
Name..	Phone......................................	E-mail...
Name..	Phone......................................	E-mail...
Name..	Phone......................................	E-mail...
Name..	Phone......................................	E-mail...
Name..	Phone......................................	E-mail...
Name..	Phone......................................	E-mail...
Name..	Phone......................................	E-mail...
Name..	Phone......................................	E-mail...
Name..	Phone......................................	E-mail...
Name..	Phone......................................	E-mail...
Name..	Phone......................................	E-mail...
Name..	Phone......................................	E-mail...